Lee Ann

Lee Ann

The Story of a Vietnamese-American Girl

TRICIA BROWN

PHOTOGRAPHS BY TED THAI

G. P. Putnam's Sons
New York

Acknowledgments

The author and photographer gratefully acknowledge the Trang family: Duong Hong Hoa, Trang Moc Tuong, Lee Ann, Jenny and Alex; the faculty and students of Bahia Vista School, especially Caroline Spiradakis, Barbara Wander, and Ruth Silverstein, Principal; The Rev. Charles Gibbs; Chaplain Shari Young; Hum Lai; Long Be Phung; Ngo Van Be; Lam Long: Lam Phung; Vitalis Pham; Nguyen Tu Quynh; Ngoc Dung Nguyen and her students; Hoa sim; Vu-Duc Vuong, Executive Director, Center for Southeast Asian Refugee Resettlement; Harriet Rohmer; Ann Hatch; Tim Hatch; William Farley; Mimi LeHot; Louis LeHot; Jacques LeHot; Noreen Coyne; Theodore Brown; Barrett Brown; and a special thank you to our editor, Refna Wilkin, for believing in us and this book.

G. P. Putnam's Sons,
a division of The Putnam & Grosset Book Group,
200 Madison Avenue, New York, NY 10016.
Published simultaneously in Canada.
Printed in the United States of America.
Book design by Jean Weiss
Map by Colleen Flis

Library of Congress Cataloging-in-Publication Data
Brown, Tricia
Lee Ann: the story of a Vietnamese-American girl/Tricia Brown:
photographs by Ted Thai. p. cm.
Summary: A young Vietnamese American girl describes her family
and school life, Saturday activities, and celebration of TET, the
Vietnamese New Year.
1. Trang, Lee Ann—Juvenile literature. 2. Vietnamese Americans—
Biography—Juvenile literature. [1. Vietnamese Americans.]
I. Thai, Ted, ill. II. Title. E184.V53T733 1991 973'.04959202—dc20
[B] 90-25708 CIP AC

ISBN 0-399-21842-4
10 9 8 7 6 5 4 3 2 1
First Impression

This book is dedicated to Barrett, Alisha, Anh, Lee Ann, Jenny, Alex—children everywhere—in hopes that they will always feel safe.

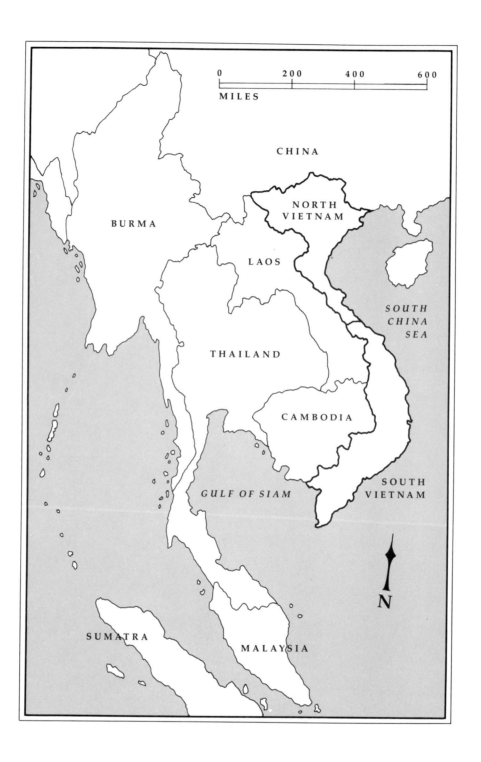

Since the fall of Saigon in 1975, Vietnamese citizens have fled their country in hopes of having a better life. These people are refugees—people who do not choose their new home as immigrants do but who are forced to leave their homeland because life for them there is no longer safe.

Thousands of refugees have left Vietnam and they continue to do so today. Those who escape by sea are called "boat people." Their journeys are always dangerous and many do not survive.

Lee Ann Trang and her parents are among these courageous people. They left their homeland and braved the seas and the first stop at the refugee camp not knowing what future awaited them.

This book is about Lee Ann's life in her new country and how she has become a Vietnamese-American girl. Now her future looks bright.

One month before I was born, my father and mother had to flee our country — Vietnam. There had been a horrible war going on there and they were not safe.

Sometimes my parents tell us the story about their escape. They were on a boat like this for twenty-one days. They remember having to hide out in a cave near the harbor until the wee hours of the morning before they could leave by boat. It was so scary!

And sad . . . we had to leave my grandmother behind but we promised we would send for her as soon as we could.

10

Soon after, I was born in the refugee camp in Malaysia where we stayed for over a year, waiting for permission to come live in the United States. When we arrived, my father's brother and his family met us.

My mother cries whenever we receive letters from our relatives left behind in our other country.

I look at our photo album with pictures our family and friends send us. My mother wants us always to remember that we come from Vietnam.

My future looks bright now. I walk to school with my friends.

The first thing I do with my third-grade class is recite:

> "I pledge allegiance to the flag of the United States of America and to the republic for which it stands, one nation, under God, indivisible, with liberty and justice for all."

Then I do my reading and learn my math.

I need some help with my English, so every day I go to ESL class. That's where kids who are new arrivals from other countries learn English as their Second Language.

I do well in school. I always pay attention to what my teacher is saying.

And I answer questions whenever I can.

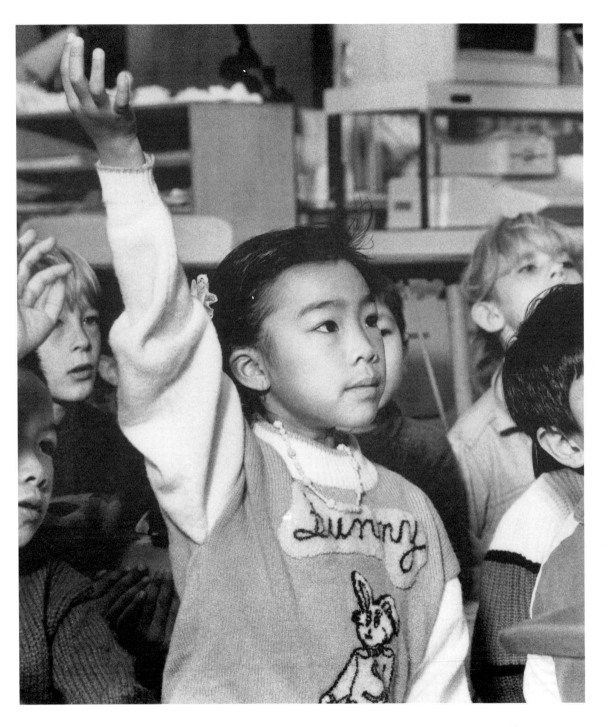

Recess is my time to play my favorite game, jump rope!

For lunch today, we have a special treat—HOT DOGS! I love them!

18

After lunch, Mr. Pham, my school's Vietnamese Community Liaison, reads a Vietnamese story to everyone in my class. He shows us the Vietnamese writing system.

At the end of the day, we have our Student of the Month Award Assembly.

Guess who is student of the month?
My school principal gives me a certificate for my good citizenship.

My parents are so proud of me!

After school, my mom makes sure Jenny and I do our homework.

24

When it is done, my friends, Lisa and Ping, come over to play. In my house, everyone takes their shoes off after they come through the door.

It takes a few seconds to microwave some popcorn for them.

I like *Thịt Chà Bông* for my snack. This is a Vietnamese food made of shredded pork.

Then, we get to play video games. I'm really good at this one . . .

On Saturdays, sometimes my father takes me to visit his best friend who is a fisherman. It's boring when I have to help repair the nets.

What I like to do best is work outside on the boat!

29

This weekend is special. My family is preparing for the Vietnamese New Year. It is called *Tết*. Our holiday is similar to Chinese New Year because Vietnam was ruled by China for hundreds of years and many of the same traditions have continued.

This is our most important celebration. It is a time for a new beginning as it marks the return of Spring.

Everyone is very happy during *Tết!*

This Saturday, one week before the holiday, we begin by cleaning our house. After we are finished, my mother and I take a drive to Chinatown to buy the special flowers, decorations, and foods.

Sunday, we help our dad decorate the house.

It takes my mom all week long to prepare the holiday foods. After school, I help her prepare *Khổ qua hầm*, a stuffed vegetable.

My dad loves them but I think they are yucky!

34

35

It is New Year's Eve at last! Before our family and guests arrive my father says a prayer.

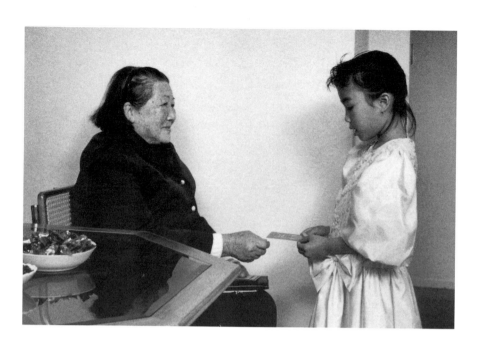

Finally, my grandmother, whom we brought over years ago, and my father's brother and his family ring our bell! My father's fisherman friend joins us, too. His wife and children are still in Vietnam, and we are hoping they will be able to come to America soon.

We children line up while Grandmother gives us special red envelopes.

Do you know what is inside them? MONEY!

Then it is time to feast. In Vietnam, we usually all eat at one table. If we don't have a table big enough for everyone, then we sit on the floor.

This evening my teacher and her husband join us for our celebration. I feel very honored.

At midnight, Daddy sets off firecrackers in front of our house to scare away evil spirits and bring us good luck all year long. Oooooh, it's noisy!

40

On New Year's Day we go to a Vietnamese Community Festival where we feed money to a dancing lion and I visit my friends, Mr. Phuc and Mr. Tran, respected elders in our community. They are wearing the traditional Vietnamese costume. It is called the *áo dài*.

I watch them perform the ancestor worship ceremony.

Finally, I attend the recital of my music school. These girls are singing Vietnamese folk songs. They are wearing costumes typical of South, Middle, and North Vietnam.

I put on my *áo dài* and my teacher helps me tune my *Đàn tranh*, a classical Vietnamese string instrument, before we give our performance.

It has been a long day for me but it has been a wonderful *Tết* celebration.

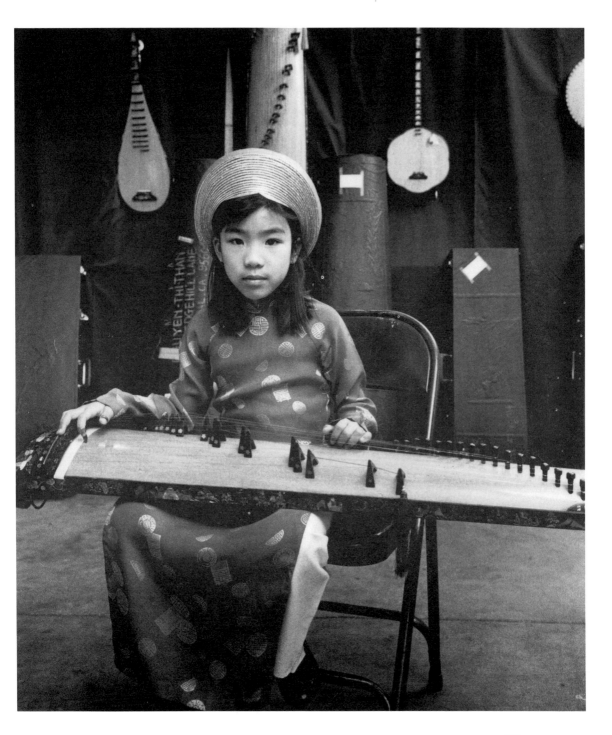

When you welcome the New Year, you are supposed to think about your past, present, and future.

I take a few moments to think about my life and then I feel good. Even though I have had some difficult times in the past, my present is happy and I think the future will be even happier.

I am proud to be a Vietnamese-American girl.

RARE